The Rock Cycle
Road Trip

MINERALS

Hit the road and discover a world that rocks!

CHERITON
CHILDREN'S BOOKS

Published in 2025 by **Cheriton Children's Books**
1 Bank Drive West, Shrewsbury, Shropshire, SY3 9DJ, UK

First Edition

Author: Sarah Eason
Designer: Paul Myerscough
Editor: Deborah Jones
Proofreader: Katie Dicker

Picture credits: Cover: Collaborate; Inside: p1: Shutterstock/PavKon, p4: Shutterstock/Eduard Goricev, p5: Shutterstock/Daniel Schreiber, p6: Shutterstock/Withan Tor, p7: Shutterstock/Ilyas Kalimullin, p8: Shutterstock/RHJPhtotos, p9: Shutterstock/Phawat, p10: Shutterstock/Aleksandr Pobedimskiy, p11: Shutterstock/Amr Hassanein, p12b: Shutterstock/Fedor Selivanov, p12t: Shutterstock/Yes058 Montree Nanta, p14: Shutterstock/DanielFreyr, p15: Shutterstock/Fotokon, p16: Shutterstock/Sanit Fuangnakhon, p17: Shutterstock/Konstantin Grosch 1986, p18: Shutterstock/I. Pilon, p19l: Shutterstock/Johan W. Elzenga, p19r: Shutterstock/Eshma, p20: Shutterstock/Shane Myers Photography, p21: Shutterstock/Asia_K, p22b: Shutterstock/AleksaStanko003, p22t: Shutterstock/Sebastian Janicki, p23: Shutterstock/Moha El-Jaw, p24: Shutterstock/Ivan Bruno de M, p25: Shutterstock/Gudkov Andrey, p26b: Shutterstock/Nada B, p26t: Shutterstock/Bjoern Wylezich, p29b: Shutterstock/Neil Lockhart, p29t: Shutterstock/Tony Baggett, p30b: Shutterstock/Neil Lockhart, p30t: Shutterstock/Bambambu, p32: Shutterstock/kksakultap, p33tl: Shutterstock/Gorodenkoff, p33tr: Shutterstock/Nik Keevil, p34: Shutterstock/GreenOak, p35b: Shutterstock/Jose Luis Stephens, p35t: Shutterstock/WH Pics, p36b: Shutterstock/Humphery, p36t: Shutterstock/Zelenskaya, p38: Shutterstock/Studio Empreinte, p39t: Shutterstock/Kreminska, p40: Shutterstock/Zhukova Valentyna, p41: Shutterstock/Angel DiBilio, p42: Shutterstock/Pornpimon Ainkaew, p43: Shutterstock/Eric Poulin.

Printed in China

CONTENTS

Chapter 1

Our Rocky World

Our planet is made almost entirely of rock. It has a small metal core at its center, but the remaining 85 percent of it is rock—and that's why it is so easy to find many amazing rocks on Earth.

All Change

Although the rocky surface of our planet may seem stable, it is being reshaped and reformed all the time. Sometimes, changes to its surface can happen quickly. For example, because of a natural disaster such as a landslide or earthquake. Most of the time, the changes to Earth's rocky surface happen very, very slowly—so slowly that we hardly notice them. Over a very long period, surface rocks are broken down to make way for new rocks. This is part of a never-ending cycle called the rock cycle.

Minerals are natural substances that are found in all rocks. Read on to find out why they play an important role in the rock cycle!

Magma is molten or semimolten rock that is full of minerals. When magma reaches Earth's surface, and cools to become hard, it still contains the minerals it held in its liquid form.

Earth's Rock Cycle

The rock cycle is a process by which one type of rock changes into another type of rock. Earth has three main types of rock: igneous rock, metamorphic rock, and sedimentary rock. Each can change into another type when affected by temperature, **weathering**, and **pressure**.

How Rock Changes

When heated deep underground, rocks turn into liquid rock. We call this melted rock magma. When rocks are worn away by weathering or erosion, they break into smaller pieces called sediment. Rock can also be squeezed under great pressure, which also forces it to change.

Understanding Rock Types

READ Here

Igneous rock is magma that has cooled and hardened. This can happen above or below the ground. Igneous rock changes by melting into magma, **eroding** into sediment, or being pressed so tightly that it becomes metamorphic rock.

Metamorphic rock began life as igneous or sedimentary rock that was then heated and squeezed. Metamorphic rock can change again by eroding into sediment or melting into magma.

Sedimentary rock is made up of squashed sediments from other rocks, plus the remains of living things. It can erode back into sediment, be squeezed into metamorphic rock, or melted into magma.

Earth is one of the four "rocky" planets of our Solar System. Also in this group are Mercury, Venus, and Mars.

Look Inside Earth

To understand the rock cycle and why rock is so affected by temperature, weathering, and pressure, we need to first look at the structure of Earth.

Earth looks solid and immovable at the surface, but inside are layers that are not at all like the surface. In fact, Earth is made up of three very different parts.

Crust: This is the outer part of our planet. It is the section on which we live. It is up to 44 miles (70 km) thick and is broken up into enormous parts, called plates.

Mantle: This mostly solid layer moves around and is about 1,800 miles (2,900 km) thick. Earth's plates float on the mantle.

Core: This is the hottest part of our planet and it forms the center of Earth. The center of the core reaches nearly 12,000 degrees Fahrenheit (6,700 °C), hot enough to keep it permanently molten, or liquid.

Rock Recycling

During the rock cycle, new rock material can rise to the surface from deep within Earth. But most surface rocks are made from existing rock that is continually recycled. For example, as a rock is weathered, a **grain** within it may be loosened. That grain may then become part of another rock. It will then be weathered and separated from that rock, then form part of a new rock, repeatedly.

Take a Rock Cycle Road Trip!

In this book, we will explore how minerals are created, the different types of minerals that exist, and why they are so important to us. We'll take an amazing rock cycle road trip to discover minerals around the world, some of the most incredible mineral sites on the planet, and how we make use of Earth's amazing minerals. So, what are you waiting for? Let's hit the road and discover a world that rocks!

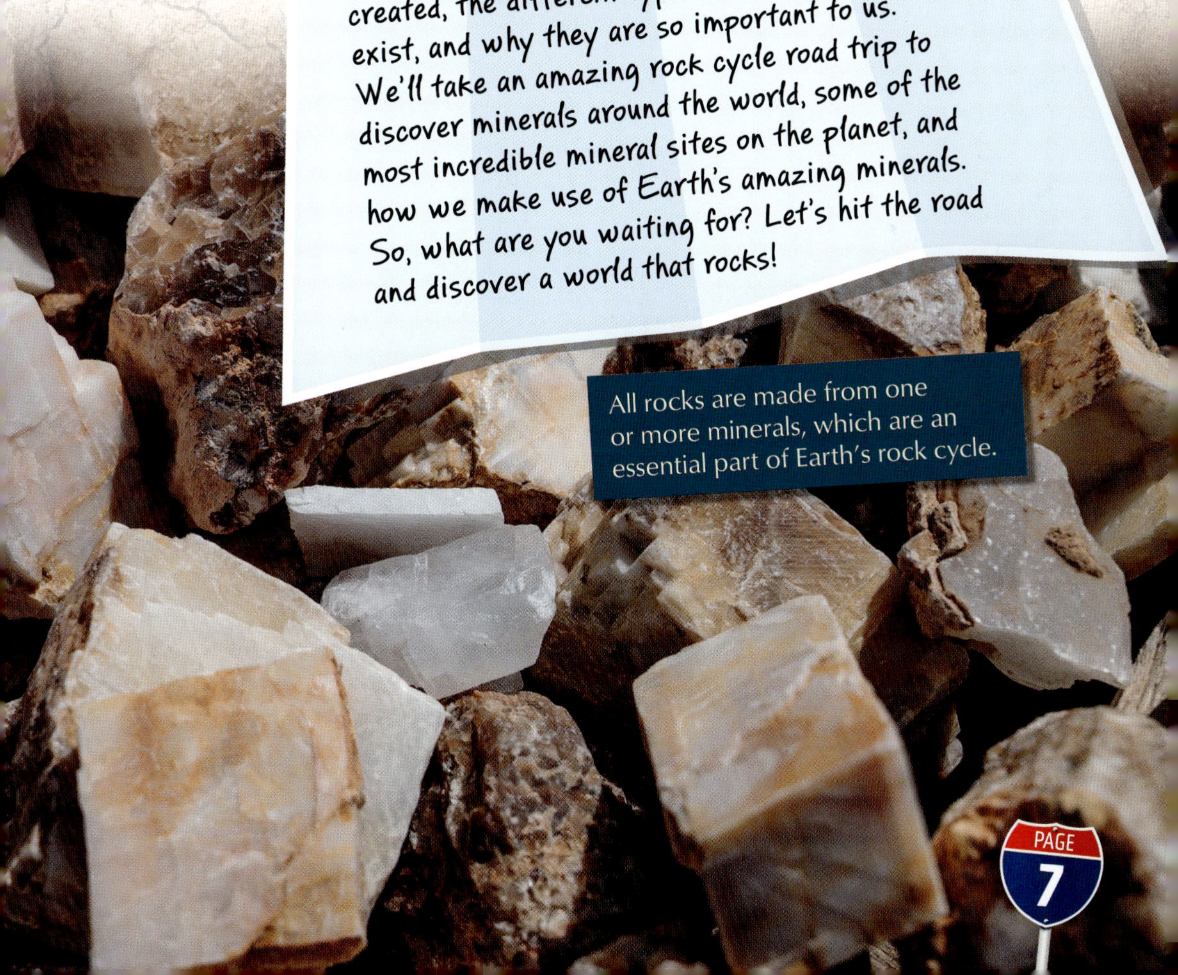

All rocks are made from one or more minerals, which are an essential part of Earth's rock cycle.

Chapter 2

A World of Minerals

Minerals are the substances that make up rocks. They are found in all rocks, from the tiny grains of sand on the shore to the high mountains that tower above the land. Minerals and rocks are used to make many of the things we need and use every day, from computers to buildings.

Made by Nature

Minerals are natural substances, formed by nature. They are not made by humans. Almost all the substances we call minerals are inorganic. That means they have never been alive and are not formed from the remains or parts of plants or animals. Minerals are found in rocks, sands, and soils. They exist on Earth's surface and deep underground.

Aluminum is shiny and useful. It is the most widely found metallic element in Earth's crust.

Gold is a very popular native element, used all over the world. It doesn't tarnish easily so it retains its beautiful shine.

Digging Deeper

The scientific study of minerals is called mineralogy, and people who study minerals are called mineralogists. They have identified thousands of minerals by looking at the chemical and physical properties of these natural substances.

Earth's Elements

Minerals are made from elements found naturally on Earth. Elements are substances that cannot be broken down into simpler substances by chemical means. Some minerals, such as copper, contain only one element: copper. They are called native elements. Other minerals are made of several elements. Quartz, for example, is a mineral made up of two elements: silicon and oxygen. Most minerals occur naturally as crystals—solid structures with flat sides and sharp edges. These special shapes may be easy to identify in their natural form, but often a mass of interlocking small crystals looks like a shapeless lump of rock.

Groups of Elements

Native elements are divided into three main groups: metals, metalloids (or semimetals), and nonmetals. These are the most widely found native metals: gold, silver, copper, platinum, mercury, lead, tin, zinc.

Minerals in the Mix

Minerals give rocks their different features, colors, and forms. The mineral crystals in most rocks are small and mixed randomly. However, sometimes crystals of single minerals, such as gold, form in the spaces in rocks to create pockets or veins.

Take a Rock Cycle Road Trip!

Minerals are fascinating, and so too are the rocks in which they are contained. Minerals determine much about a rock's features, for example, how light or heavy it is. **Archeologists** study rocks used to create buildings to find out more about life in the past. The rocks that were used to build the impressive pyramids in ancient Egypt tell us a lot about how they may have been made. Egypt is the first stop on our road trip. Head this way!

ROCK STOP! EGYPT, AFRICA

The limestone pyramids of ancient Egypt often had pink granite pillars and roof blocks. The limestone that the Egyptian builders used was dragged from nearby **quarries**. The rock formed from ancient sedimentary **deposits** of the Nile River, which dumped layer upon layer of sand, shells, and other **organic matter** over thousands of years on the surrounding land. The granite was brought from far away. As granite is very heavy, it must have been brought by boat up the Nile River and required many workers to move it.

Granite rock contains dense minerals such as feldspar and biotite, which is partly why it is so heavy.

Common and Uncommon

Around 30 percent of all minerals are silicates, making them Earth's most common type of mineral. Silicates include rocks such as quartz and clay, which contain silicon and oxygen. More than 90 percent of the mass of Earth's crust is made up of silicates. The remaining minerals make up a group called nonsilicates. There are many important nonsilicates on Earth, and they include carbonates, halides, oxides, and sulfides.

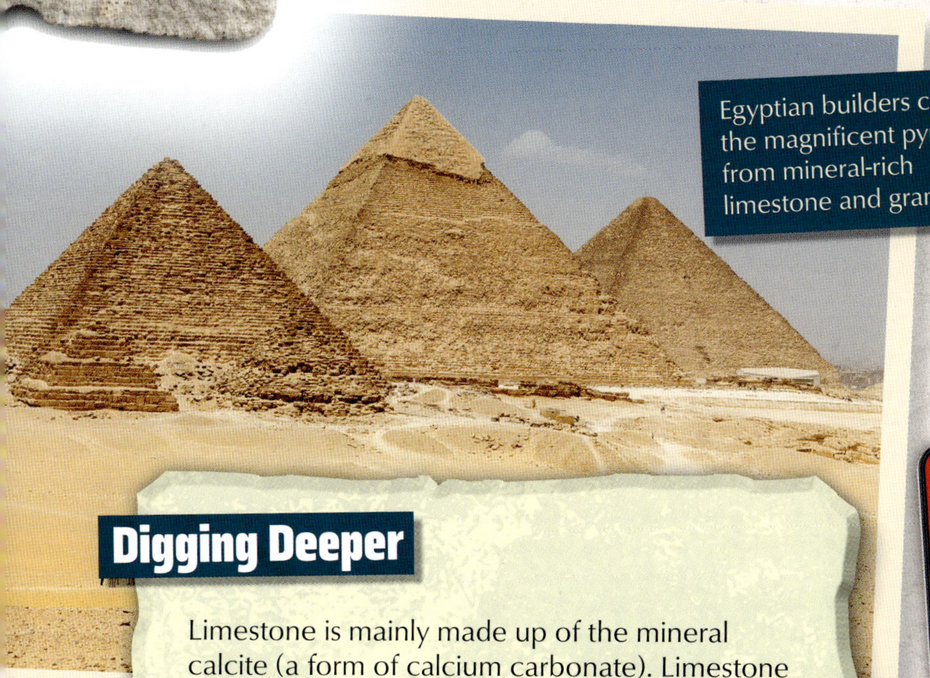

Egyptian builders created the magnificent pyramids from mineral-rich limestone and granite.

Digging Deeper

Limestone is mainly made up of the mineral calcite (a form of calcium carbonate). Limestone forms from the shells and skeletons of marine animals such as coral, shellfish, and algae, which are rich in calcium carbonate. Over millions of years, layers of these shells and skeletons become compressed and harden into limestone rock, or they can **dissolve** in seawater and form limestone when the water **evaporates**.

READ Here

CALCITE

What a Rock Star!

Calcite is a mineral found in many rocks around the world, including sedimentary, metamorphic, and igneous rocks. It is called a "ubiquitous mineral," because it is a mineral that is found all over Earth.

Rock Star Characteristics

- Pale white, chalky white, or light gray
- Quite shiny
- Not hard, easily scratched

THAT ROCKS!

Calcite is used in many medicines. It is mixed with sugar and flavorings to make chewable tablets that can help people who suffer from digestive problems such as an overly **acidic** stomach.

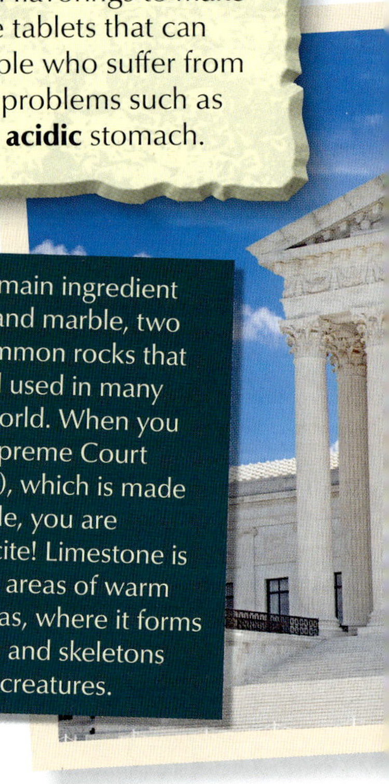

Calcite is the main ingredient of limestone and marble, two extremely common rocks that are found and used in many parts of the world. When you look at the Supreme Court building (right), which is made of white marble, you are looking at calcite! Limestone is often found in areas of warm oceans and seas, where it forms from the shells and skeletons of ancient sea creatures.

Take a Rock Cycle Road Trip!

Calcite Hotspots

Calcite is found all over the world, most notably in these places:

Did You Know?

Calcite is used to help repair the **environment** in places where it has been damaged by chemicals due to industry. For example, calcium-containing limestone is added to streams and rivers that have been polluted by industrial chemicals, to help **neutralize** the water.

Chapter 3

Making Minerals

Although minerals can form anywhere on Earth, most of the minerals in the rocks that make up Earth's crust come from deep beneath the ground. They reach the surface when magma from below moves upward.

Rising and Falling

Magma is constantly rising and falling below Earth's crust. As magma warms it becomes lighter and rises slowly as it escapes the pull of gravity. When it travels toward Earth's surface, it gets cooler and denser, or heavier. This causes it to gradually fall. As the magma cools, the melted minerals in it become solid and form crystals.

In some places, magma bursts suddenly through Earth's crust when a volcano **erupts**. On Earth's surface, magma is called lava. As lava cools, the molten minerals inside it harden and form igneous rock.

Digging Deeper

Geodes are hollow rocks that contain crystals. In igneous rock, geodes begin as air bubbles within lava that cools. In sedimentary rock, rainwater can dissolve parts of the rock to form a hollow space. As groundwater seeps into these spaces over millions of years, the minerals dissolved in the water gradually form crystals on the inside of the hollow rock.

READ Here

How Minerals Form

The way in which minerals form depends mainly on the environment in which they are created. Sometimes minerals dissolve in hot water, for example, and are transported wherever the water travels—through holes and cracks in rocks and across land. As the water cools, the dissolved minerals and other elements crystallize to form new minerals, which become deposited in the spaces within rocks.

The mineral halite, which is used as table salt, forms when water evaporates in a hot, shallow part of an ocean. As it evaporates, the salt the water contains is left behind.

Minerals from Space

Mineralogists have found minerals that were not formed on Earth—they are **extraterrestrial**! **Meteoroids** are rocks that fly through space and sometimes crash into Earth (as meteorites), bringing minerals to our planet.

Arriving on Earth

Meteoroids formed in space at the same time as Earth and other planets. When meteorites hit Earth, they break up and the minerals that formed them become part of Earth's crust. Kamacite, which contains the element iron, is one of the minerals that arrived on Earth in meteoroids.

By studying the minerals of meteorites, we can learn more about how the planets they came from formed and what they may be like.

How Old Is Earth?

Scientists use minerals from meteorites to estimate the age of Earth. Meteoroids and Earth formed at the same time, but the rocks in Earth's crust are constantly being created, changed, and destroyed as part of the rock cycle. Most iron meteoroids stay the same, so by learning how old they are, scientists can discover Earth's age too: more than 4.5 billion years!

Digging Deeper

When meteorite rocks are polished they reveal beautiful patterns of lines called Widmanstätten patterns. The lines are named after the man who discovered them in 1808. These patterns are formed from crisscrossing lines of crystals that developed as meteoroids slowly cooled.

READ Here

Take a Rock Cycle *Road Trip!*

Did you know that meteoroids fall to Earth every year? In fact, each year thousands of meteoroids that weigh more than 1 pound (450 g) fall to our planet. Luckily, most of them fall into the oceans or onto deserts. Many fall in Antarctica, a vast wilderness of snow and ice. It's the next stop on our road trip.

ROCK STOP! ANTARCTICA

The huge frozen expanse of Antarctica in Earth's southern hemisphere is a hotspot for meteorites. To date, scientists have found about 45,000 meteorites there. The minerals found in meteorites are very rare on Earth. Minerals often found in meteorites are moissanite, schreibersite, and xifengite.

Scientists believe that as many as 300,000 more mineral-rich meteorites may lie hidden in the snow and ice of Antarctica.

METEORITE
What a Rock Star!

Meteorites are fascinating insights to the world of space. They tell us what planets and other space objects may be made of, and are important clues to the Universe's dramatic past.

Rock Star Characteristics

- Often black in color
- Usually heavy for their size, because they contain dense minerals
- Often **magnetic**, because they contain iron, which is metallic

THAT ROCKS!

One enormous meteorite named the Canyon Diablo landed on Earth about 50,000 years ago. It hit what is now Arizona, forming a crater that measures about 0.75 miles (1.2 km) across and is nearly 600 feet (180 m) deep. About 30 tonnes (27 mt) of meteorite fragments, or pieces, from the impact were scattered across the area. The meteorite contained the minerals iron and nickel, which are also some of the minerals that are found in Earth's crust.

Take a

Rock Cycle Road Trip!

Meteorite Hotspots

Meteorites have been found on every **continent** of the world!

Did You Know?

Around 400 pieces of the Moon have been discovered on Earth. We know that these meteorites came from the Moon because they are like rocks that were brought back to Earth after the Apollo 17 mission to the Moon, which took place in 1972.

Meteorites fall all over Earth, but they are often found in very cold or hot places, such as Arizona (left). The lack of rainfall and vegetation there helps preserve the meteorites and makes them easier to find.

Chapter 4

Studying Minerals

Minerals form all the rocks on Earth: igneous, sedimentary, and metamorphic. We know that during the rock cycle these three types of rock change form, and as they do so the minerals within the rocks are recycled over very long periods of time.

Changing Form

Igneous rocks form when the minerals that make up magma cool and harden. Particles on the surface of igneous rocks are weathered by rain, ice, and wind. Water and wind then erode these pieces of sediment somewhere new. The sediments pile up and press together to form sedimentary rock. Heat and pressure underground can rearrange elements in sedimentary rocks to form new minerals and new rocks—metamorphic rocks.

Volcanic areas such as the Hawaiian Islands have a lot of igneous rocks, which formed when magma from the islands' volcanoes cooled and hardened.

Sedimentary rocks are treasure troves, full of clues to the past. This rock contains the fossilized skeleton of a sea turtle.

Known for Minerals

Certain minerals are often found in particular rock types. For example, granite is a well-known igneous rock. It contains the minerals feldspar, quartz, mica, and amphibole. Feldspar, calcite, iron, and magnesium are often found in basalt and gabbro rocks, which are also igneous rocks. Both igneous and metamorphic rocks often contain a group of minerals known as amphiboles. Sedimentary rocks often contain calcite, dolomite, gypsum, and halite.

Minerals Making Fossils

Sedimentary rocks often contain fossils. When sea animals die and sink to the ocean floor, water carrying tiny pieces of sediment gradually soaks into their empty shells. Over time, minerals from the water replace the minerals that make up the shell. These minerals turn into rock that is the same shape as the shell, creating a fossil.

Digging Deeper

Pumice is a type of igneous rock that forms when lava cools slowly. It often contains feldspar, augite, hornblende, and zircon minerals. If pumice is found at a particular location, it is evidence, or proof, that there was a volcano in that region in the past. The age of the pumice tells scientists roughly when the eruption happened.

READ Here

Thousands of Minerals

There are more than 5,000 different types of minerals, and more are being discovered all the time. Some minerals look similar, so **geologists** have figured out different ways to identify them all. They can be divided into metals and nonmetals, and identified by their hardness, color, and how shiny they are.

Clues in Colors

Some minerals can be identified by their color. Azurite is always deep blue. Others, such as fluorite, come in several different colors. Fluorite must be identified by other features, such as its hardness and the way in which it breaks. When split, fluorite often breaks into pieces that are the shape of an octahedron.

Azurite (top) has a stunning blue color and malachite (left) is a rich, vibrant green.

Copper Clues

Malachite is an unusual and beautiful mineral containing light and dark green bands of color. Malachite tells us that the metal mineral copper was in the area in the past, and might still be found nearby today. This is because malachite forms after hot water dissolves copper from underground rock.

Clues in Shine

Some minerals are identified by their luster, or shininess. Quartz and gold both reflect light better than other minerals so appear to shine. Some minerals come in a range of colors but can be identified because they always look the same color when ground to a powder. We call this their "streak." For example, calcite comes in many different colors and shapes, but when crushed it is always white.

Identifying Minerals

Mineralogists also use other markers to identify minerals, including:

- Cleavage: this describes how a mineral breaks into pieces. Some minerals break into small cubelike shapes, others break into thin sheets
- Specific Gravity (SG): this is a measurement of the density of a mineral

Digging Deeper

Iron pyrite is called "fool's gold" because this mineral has a similar luster and color to gold. In fact, they look so similar that some people have been fooled into thinking this cheap and common mineral really is gold!

Iron pyrite looks amazingly like gold—no wonder people have been fooled by it!

Common and Rare

Some minerals are very common. For example, quartz is found in desert sand and on seashores all over the world. Other minerals, such as gold, are rare and only found in certain places.

Different Values

Minerals such as quartz and feldspar make up more than half of Earth's crust. They are easily found and exist in large quantities in a lot of places. That is why they are not valued as greatly as rare minerals that are only found in specific places. Gold is found in small amounts in rocks around the world, but there are larger amounts in certain countries, such as South Africa. Red beryl is a very rare mineral. So far it has only been found in parts of Utah and New Mexico.

Digging Deeper

READ Here

When scientists discovered the mineral ringwoodite trapped inside a diamond, it gave them important clues about the structure of our planet. The diamond contained bright blue ringwoodite, which only forms at 250 to 400 miles (400 to 640 km) beneath Earth's surface and had water trapped within it. Deep-seated volcanic eruptions had carried the diamond to Earth's surface. Scientists say this finding suggests there may be several times the amount of water inside our planet than in the oceans!

Take a Rock Cycle Road Trip!

Not only does mining harm animals and plants—the people who mine the mineral often work in terrible conditions.

Coltan is a black, tar-like mineral that is very good at holding and moving electrical signals. That is why it is used in cell phones, computers, and a wide range of other electronic devices. It is quite rare and only found in a small number of places. Almost half of the coltan used around the world comes from Central Africa. That's the next stop on our road trip.

ROCK STOP! DEMOCRATIC REPUBLIC OF THE CONGO (DRC), AFRICA

The Democratic Republic of the Congo (DRC) in central Africa is very rich in **natural resources**. In fact, all the combined mineral resources of the DRC, including diamonds, cobalt, gold, and zinc, are worth an estimated $24 trillion. The area is particularly rich in deposits of the mineral coltan, which is used in the manufacture of electronic devices. It is heavily mined in the DRC.

Mining in the DRC has damaged the natural environment, unfortunately, harming **ecosystems** that include already threatened animals such as the mountain gorilla.

COLTAN

What a Rock Star!

The name coltan is short for columbite-tantalite, which are the two important minerals that coltan is made up of. When it is ground, coltan becomes a heat-resistant powder, which can store electrical charges. That is why it is so widely used to make electronic devices.

Rock Star Characteristics

- Black in color
- Dull, non-shiny surface
- Not an abundant resource, so very valuable

Did You Know?

Coltan is a controversial resource because mining it causes damage to the environment but also because of the mining techniques typically used to extract coltan. It is often mined by hand by poorly paid workers, including children. Wars over coltan have also broken out in some of the countries where it is mined, including the DRC and Brazil.

Take a Rock Cycle Road Trip!

Coltan Hotspots

Precious coltan is found in these areas worldwide:

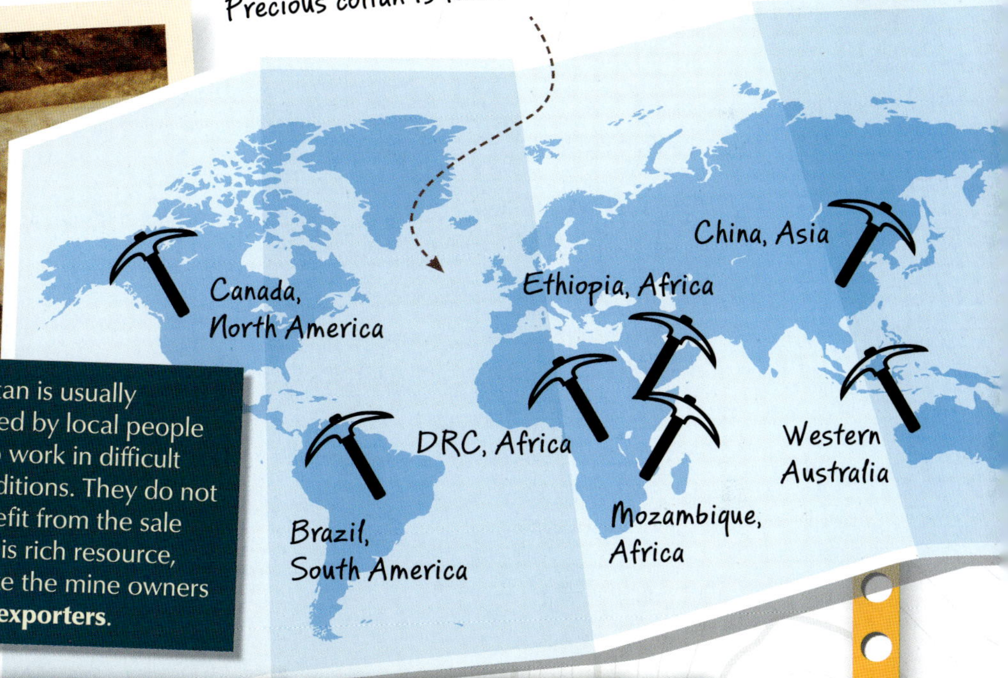

Coltan is usually mined by local people who work in difficult conditions. They do not benefit from the sale of this rich resource, unlike the mine owners and **exporters**.

THAT ROCKS!

Tantalum, one of the elements that makes up coltan, is used to make surgical appliances as well as electronic materials. When inserted in the human body, the **immune system** does not react to tantalum. That makes it an ideal material to use for bone replacement, binding damaged muscles, or connecting torn **nerves**.

Chapter 5

Using Minerals

Mining minerals can be expensive, so before work begins, companies hire a geologist to figure out whether there are high-quality minerals or metals in a location. Geologists drill holes and collect material from inside Earth, which they study to figure out if the area contains enough minerals to make it worth mining.

Getting to Minerals

Mining for minerals is done in several ways. Minerals found near Earth's surface can be extracted using an open pit mining method. During this process, workers dig a pit in Earth's surface to reach the rocks. Other minerals are hidden deep inside Earth. They are removed by digging a deep shaft, or tunnel, straight down into the ground. Minerals that are removed from Earth are called **ores**.

READ Here

Digging Deeper

In the past, people panned for gold. They washed gravel in a pan to separate out pieces of gold. The gold grains they found told them whether a bigger source of gold was nearby. Rough grains with hard edges suggest that a source of gold is nearby. Grains become smooth when they are eroded over long distances, so the smoother the grains of gold, the farther away the source.

Take a
Rock Cycle *Road Trip!*

Gold has always inspired people with excitement, and never more so than during the California Gold Rush that took place between 1848 and 1855. Let's head to California and find out more about its gold rush.

ROCK STOP! **CALIFORNIA, NORTH AMERICA**

The California Gold Rush was inspired after James W. Marshall found gold on January 24, 1848, at Sutter's Mill near Coloma, California. News of his gold find spread quickly, and soon 300,000 people had traveled to California from across the United States and overseas in search of glittering gold.

During the Gold Rush, people claimed land next to rivers and used pans like this one to wash gravel that might contain gold.

GOLD

What a Rock Star!

Gold is one of the most precious resources in the world and is highly prized for its beautiful color. It also has many different uses in our lives.

Rock Star Characteristics

- Golden in color, but can vary from golden to yellow
- Has a shiny luster
- Easily cut and shaped

The Nevada Gold Mines are the biggest producer of gold in the world. This complex of five gold mines accounts for about 75 percent of annual gold production in the United States.

THAT ROCKS!

Most gold is used in the production of jewelry. Much of the rest is used to make coins, bars of gold, electronics, medicine, computers, and other tools and goods.

Did You Know?

Gold is mined on every continent on Earth except Antarctica. Scientists believe there may be huge amounts of gold on the continent, but mining gold there is banned.

Take a Rock Cycle Road Trip!

Gold Hotspots

Most of the gold discovered to date has been found in just three countries:

Minerals in Our World

People use minerals every day and in many ways. Minerals provide the materials to create the buildings we live in, the magazines we read, and the cell phones we rely on. The world would simply not be the same without minerals.

Everyday Minerals

Rocks cut from the land make our buildings. Slate is sliced into pieces to make roof tiles and granite slabs are used for countertops. Some minerals are crushed and mixed with other substances to make building materials. For example, clay minerals are used to make bricks and floor tiles. Quartz from sand is used to make glass, and kaolinite is used to make paper, mugs, and toilets.

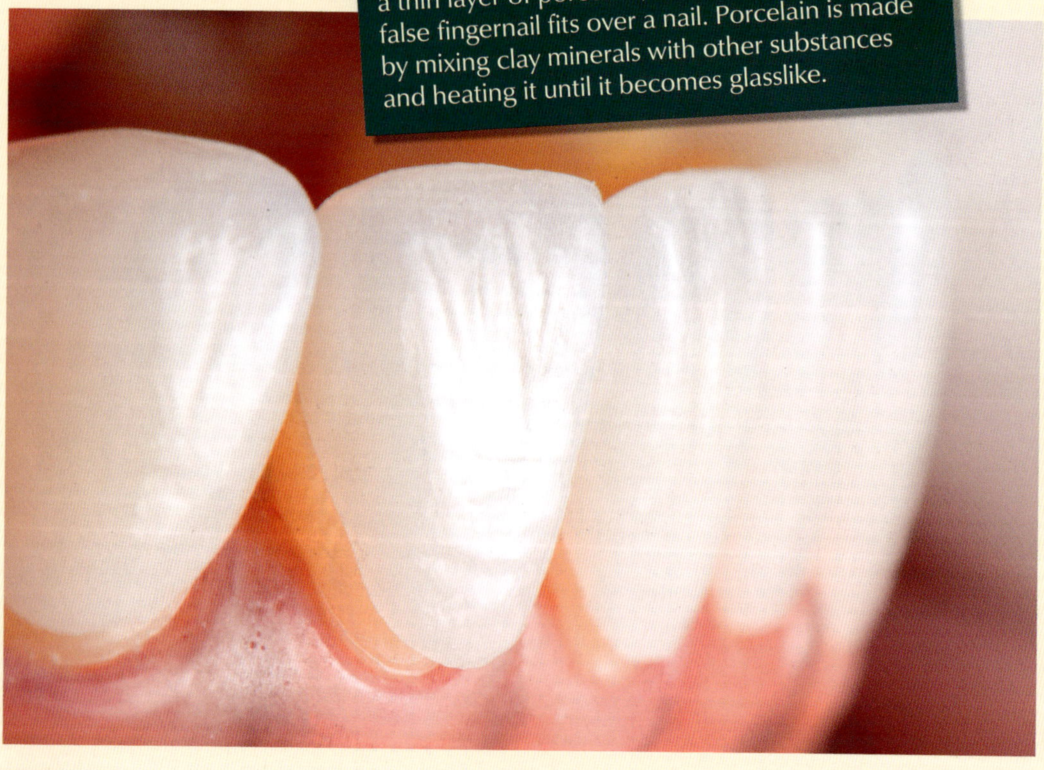

When a tooth is damaged it can be covered with a thin layer of porcelain, in the same way that a false fingernail fits over a nail. Porcelain is made by mixing clay minerals with other substances and heating it until it becomes glasslike.

People have been using Earth's precious minerals for thousands of years. Tools such as these made from flint were made many centuries ago, but have lasted to this day. They are important clues to the past.

Hard, Solid, and Long-Lasting

Minerals are hard and solid and can last a long time in rock form, which is why we have evidence of how people used minerals in the past. Flint is a type of quartz that is colored by the other minerals found within it. It can be cut to give a very sharp edge. Tools and weapons made from flint have been found that date from prehistoric times. The types of tools we find and how well-used they are tell us much about how people lived in the past.

Digging Deeper

By striking a flint pebble, early man could create two halves. Each had quite a flat surface, which, when tapped lightly, could be broken into different-sized flakes. Primitive man used these flakes as knives. Pieces of flint could also be used as scrapers, for removing animal skin, for example. Flint is very durable, or tough and long-lasting, which made it a prized material for tool-making in early human history.

Made by Minerals

Metals are very useful minerals. They allow us to make many different things, from airplanes, ships, and buildings, to cans and jewelry. Each metal has its own particular properties. Some metals are extremely hard and some can be bent and shaped much more easily. For example, aluminum is used to make cans because it is light and easy to shape.

Most of the iron we refine is used to make steel. Steel is very strong, light, and easily shaped for making ships, saucepans, and building frames, for example.

Electricity to Jewelry

Electricity moves easily through copper, which makes copper metal perfect for use in electrical wires. Engineers have been using copper in electronics for many years. Some precious metals, such as gold, are also good at conducting electricity. They are sometimes used in electronics, but because they are expensive, they're more often used for jewelry and expensive watches.

Digging Deeper

When people discovered that some heavy stones did not flake or fracture when they were hit, but instead were soft and stayed intact as their shapes altered, their relationship with minerals changed forever. People had discovered that metals such as copper and iron could be used as tools, and were far superior to the stone tools they had been using.

One of the earliest metals to be used for making tools was copper, because it can be found in rocks as a pure element. It was hammered into sheets, divided into strips, and then separated into pieces. These pieces were then shaped into arrowheads, knives, and choppers. Later, people discovered that iron too could be manipulated into shapes.

READ Here

Take a Rock Cycle Road Trip!

More copper is produced on the continent of South America than anywhere else on Earth, and it's the next stop on our road trip. Head this way!

ROCK STOP! CHILE, SOUTH AMERICA

Chile is the biggest producer of copper in the world. The country produces about 6 million tonnes (5.4 million mt) of copper every year. Closely following Chile is Peru, also in South America, which produces about 2.5 million tonnes (2.3 million mt) of copper every year.

Early man shaped copper by beating pieces of it into holes in rocks to mold them. Copper weapons have been found dating from between 7,000 and 10,000 years ago. By about 500 BCE, people were widely using and working with iron.

Copper is extracted from this large mine in Chile.

COPPER

What a Rock Star!

Alongside gold, copper is the only metal with a natural color that isn't silver or gray. Copper is often found in wirelike strands or as lumps called nuggets.

Rock Star Characteristics

- Reddish-orange in color, but can also be brown or gray
- Shiny, and reflects light easily
- Can be easily shaped and cut

In Asia, China is the biggest producer of copper, and it is also the world's biggest consumer, or user, of copper, using 54 percent of all Earth's **refined** copper.

Take a
Rock Cycle Road Trip!

Did You Know?

When copper is exposed to moisture and air for a long time, it forms a thin protective coating with a greenish color.

Copper Hotspots

Here are some of the places in the world where copper is mined:

THAT ROCKS!

Copper gets its name from the island of Cyprus! The Romans got their copper from Cyprus in the Mediterannean Sea, and called it *cuprium*, then *cuprum*, after their name for the island. It later became known as "copper" in English.

Chapter 6

Minerals for Life

Minerals not only make up the rocks of our planet, they are also needed by living things. When rocks are broken down in the rock cycle, the minerals become part of the soil. Plants take in minerals from soil through their roots. Animals take in minerals when they eat plants or plant-eating animals.

Phosphates for Plants

Plants need a group of minerals called phosphates, which help the plants grow. That is one reason why plants grow well on soil near volcanoes, where minerals blasted from the volcano have become part of the soil. Farmers can also add fertilizers, which contain minerals, to soil to help plants grow.

Minerals for Health

When animals, including humans, eat plants, or plant-eating animals, they get minerals from that food. For example, beef contains the mineral iron, which is important for making healthy blood, and milk contains calcium, which helps build healthy bones and teeth.

Many marine animals need calcium to build strong, tough shells.

Good sources of iron include beans, lentils, apricots, spinach, meat, and pumpkin seeds.

Major and Minor

The amount of minerals the human body needs varies, but larger amounts of major minerals are needed than minor minerals. Major minerals include calcium, phosphorous, potassium, sulfur, sodium, chloride, and magnesium. Minor minerals include iron, zinc, copper, and manganese.

Strong and Healthy

Calcium is required for strong and healthy bones. Without the mineral, bones become weak and brittle, or easily break. Calcium also helps keep the heart and muscles healthy. Iodine helps keep an important body part called the thyroid working, and also keeps the **metabolism** healthy. It is also important in brain health. Iron helps with the transportation of oxygen in blood, and helps the immune system fight infection.

Digging Deeper

Most animals that have hard shells covering their bodies, such as shellfish and snails, need the **chemical compound** calcium carbonate to build their shells.

READ Here

Minerals in Everything

Minerals are our planet! They form all of Earth's rocks and sediments and are important parts of soil. But because we rarely think about them, we often take minerals for granted. We don't stop to think that the sidewalks we walk on, the roads we drive on, the buildings we live and work in, and the food we eat all contain minerals.

Minerals Are Precious

Minerals take millions of years to form so when we remove them from the ground and use them, they cannot easily be replaced. Some of the devices we use also require rare minerals to work, and these are even harder to replace. Mining is also destructive because it destroys habitats where plants and animals live and can pollute the land and water around them.

Recycle and Reuse

Recycling is one way of reducing the amount of minerals the world uses. To recycle an object, it is broken up and the minerals in it are used to make new products. For example, the steel in cars can be recycled and used to make new cars. Aluminum cans are melted and reshaped into new cans. Computers and other electronic devices are recycled so the metals inside them, including copper and gold, can be used again. Minerals matter, so think about how much you use and how much you can recycle too.

If we take care to protect Earth's incredible rock cycle, and the precious minerals that are such an important part of it, we will continue to find and use minerals for years to come.

Without minerals, life on Earth would be impossible.

Digging Deeper

Identifying and understanding rocks and minerals here on Earth, and discovering how they formed, helps us learn about the past on other planets, such as Mars. A group of minerals called phyllosilicates have been found on Mars. These minerals are a little like clay and form in wet places on Earth. If phyllosilicates also exist on Mars, that means there must have been water on the planet in the past.

READ Here

Minerals Forever?

We need to take care when we make use of Earth's amazing minerals, and use them wisely. If we use too much of our planet's precious minerals, too quickly, we could run out of this vital resource.

The Road Trip Guide to Mineral Hunting

A magnifying glass can help you see the detail in a rock. Try to use a glass that provides five to ten times magnification so you can clearly see your **specimen** up close.

Had a great road trip? Loved the book? Want to try out rock and mineral hunting yourself? Awesome! Here's an easy guide that will explain the basics. The great thing about hunting for minerals and rocks is that anyone can do it and it costs very little. All you need is a pair of sharp eyes and some resources such as books and websites to help you identify the rocks and minerals you find. A few key pieces of kit help too.

Rock and Mineral Hunting Tools

The rock and mineral hunter's most important tools are a hammer and chisel—and it's worth investing in some proper **geological** ones. The hammer should mostly be used for splitting stones, and not for breaking stones from cliff faces.

IMPORTANT CLUES

You will need to use a detailed mineral-identifying guide when searching for minerals. Compare the minerals you find against your guide to help you identify them. Remember to look at the key features that help mineralogists determine what mineral they may be looking at, as discussed on pages 22–23 of this book. If you think you have found a mineral, follow these steps:

- Wipe away any dirt with a cloth so you can examine the sample more clearly with your magnifying glass. You could try scratching the sample against an unglazed white tile. Compare this "streak" color with the minerals in your identifying guide.
- If you are lucky enough to have found a mineral, give it a scrub with an old toothbrush and some water, then dry it. Then look at it again and compare it to pictures in your mineral identifying guide to figure out what type of mineral it is.

Discovering minerals in rocks is incredibly exciting!

Keep Safe!

Rocks can be sharp, heavy, and hard, and the places where you find them may be dangerous, so it's very important to keep safe. Try to rock and mineral hunt in a group and take an adult with you. Rocks can splinter when hit, so always wear goggles when hammering. Tough gloves are useful and a helmet is also important for protection if working near places where rocks could fall.

The Rock Cycle Road Trip QUIZ

How much have you learned about minerals, the rock cycle, and our amazing planet on your road trip? Take the quiz and find out!

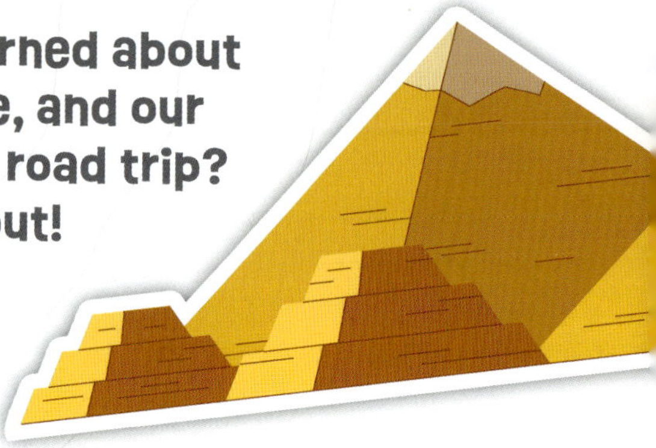

1. Where are minerals found in nature?

2. Why are minerals inorganic?

3. Why is granite heavy?

4. What is the main mineral in limestone?

5. What mineral forms when seawater evaporates?

6. What does the human body use iron for?

7. What is fool's gold?

8. What are space rocks called when they're found on Earth?

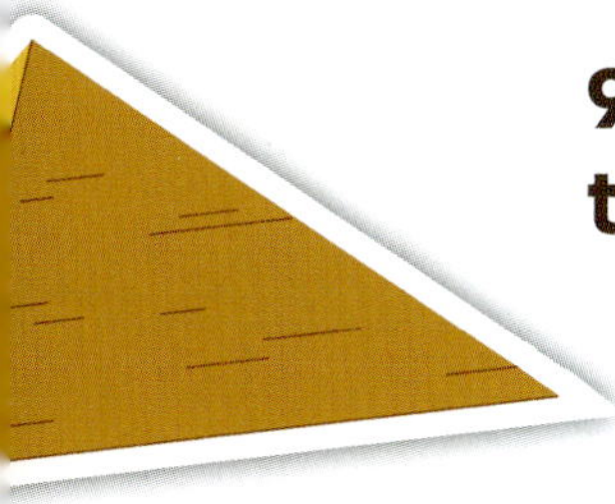

9. What country produces the most copper?

10. What is coltan used for?

ANSWERS

1. In rocks, sand, and soil
2. They do not come from a plant or animal
3. It contains dense minerals such as feldspar and biotite
4. Calcite
5. Halite (rock salt)
6. Iron helps with the transportation of oxygen in blood, and helps the immune system fight infection
7. Iron pyrite
8. Meteorites
9. Chile
10. Making electronic devices

GLOSSARY

acidic having the properties of an acid—a chemical substance that can react with other substances to form salts. Some acids burn or dissolve the substances they come into contact with

archeologists scientists who study the material remains of past human activities

chemical compound a chemical substance that is made up of two or more elements

continent a continuous expanse of land on Earth. The seven continents are Asia, Africa, North America, South America, Antarctica, Europe, and Oceania

deposits places where particular minerals, crystals, or gemstones have formed

dissolve when a solid mixes with a liquid and becomes part of it, to make a solution

ecosystems all the living things in particular areas and the way they interact with each other and with the environment

electrical charges when things hold or carry electricity

environment the natural world, as a whole or in a particular geographical area

eroding wearing away. Rocks can be worn away and transported by natural forces such as wind or water

erupts suddenly bursts out, such as the eruption of molten rock from a volcano

evaporates turns from a liquid into a gas

exporters sellers of goods to another country

extraterrestrial something that originates from outside Earth or its atmosphere

geological relating to the study of Earth's physical structure

geologists scientists who study Earth and what it is made of

grain a mineral crystal or sediment particle that makes up rock

immune system a network of cells, tissues, and organs that help the body fight infection

magnetic an object that is attracted to a magnet, or a metal object that attracts other objects containing iron or steel

metabolism the chemical reactions in the body's cells that change food into energy

meteoroids small rocky objects orbiting the Sun. When meteoroids hit Earth, they are called meteorites

natural resources supplies of something found naturally on Earth that can be used for a particular purpose

nerves fibers that carry signals between the brain or spinal cord and other parts of the body

neutralize to counteract the effect of something, such as making a substance less acidic

ores natural rocks or sediment that contain a metal or valuable mineral that can be extracted and sold

organic matter carbon-based compounds found in nature that come from the remains of living things, such as plants and animals

pressure a continuous physical force exerted on an object by something it is in contact with. Pressure increases underground, for example, because of the downward push of rock above

quarries large, deep pits from which stone or other materials are extracted

refined when unwanted substances have been removed through processing

specimen a piece of a mineral (or plant or animal) that is used as an example of its type (or species) for further study

weathering the wearing away of a substance over time because of the effects of sunlight, wind, water, or other weather conditions

FIND OUT MORE

Books

DK. *Rock & Mineral* (DK Eyewitness). DK Children, 2020.

Griffin, Annabel. *Rocks and Fossils—One Planet*. Hungry Tomato, 2022.

National Geographic Kids. *Rocks and Minerals* (Ultimate Explorer Field Guides). National Geographic Kids, 2019.

Woolf, Alex. *The Science of Rocks and Minerals: The Hard Truth About the Stuff Beneath Our Feet*. Scholastic, 2018.

Websites

Take another look at the rock cycle at:
www.cotf.edu/ete/modules/msese/earthsysflr/rock.html

Find out more about minerals at:
www.ducksters.com/science/earth_science/minerals.php

Learn more about minerals at:
kids.britannica.com/kids/article/mineral/353468

Learn all about minerals, crystals, and other aspects of rocks at:
www.mineralogy4kids.org

Publisher's note to educators and parents:
All the websites featured above have been carefully reviewed to ensure that they are suitable for students. However, many websites change often, and we cannot guarantee that a site's future contents will continue to meet our high standards of educational value. Please be advised that students should be closely monitored whenever they access the Internet.

INDEX

ABOUT THE AUTHOR

Sarah Eason has written many books for children on a wide variety of topics, from history to geography and science. She would love to take a rock cycle road trip and visit some of the amazing rocky places explored in this book.